# POETRY
## from THE
# AMICUS
# JOURNAL

**THE AMICUS JOURNAL** is a publication of the
**Natural Resources Defense Council** (NRDC), a
nonprofit membership organization founded in 1970
and dedicated to protecting natural resources and to
improving the quality of the human environment.
With 140,000 members and a staff of lawyers,
scientists, and environmental specialists, NRDC com-
bines the power of law, the power of science, and the
power of people in defense of the environment.
*Amicus* ( ə mē′ kəs) is Latin for "friend." Its most
common usage is in the phrase *amicus curiae,* which
means "friend of the court," a role NRDC has played
on many occasions as an advocate for the environment.

# POETRY
## from THE
## AMICUS
## JOURNAL

Edited by Brian Swann
and Peter Borrelli

Introduction by
Brian Swann

Designed and Illustrated by
Andrea Hendrick

 Tioga Publishing Company
Palo Alto, California

The poems in this anthology originally appeared in *The Amicus Journal*. For permission to reprint them, grateful acknowledgment is made to each author. Further acknowledgment is made to the holders of copyright and publishers of the following poems:

"Spring," "The Pipefish," and "Five A.M. in the Pinewoods," by Mary Oliver from her *House of Light*. Copyright ©1990 by Mary Oliver. Reprinted by permission of Beacon Press.

"The Idea of Balance Is to Be Found in Herons and Loons," by Jim Harrison, from his *The Theory & Practice of Rivers and New Poems*. Reprinted by permission of Clark City Press.

"Return," by John Daniel, from his *Common Ground*. Copyright ©1988 by John Daniel. Reprinted by permission of Confluence Press.

"A Life," by Philip Booth, from his *Relations: Selected Poems 1950-1985*. Copyright ©1986 by Viking Penguin. Reprinted by permission of Philip Booth.

"Silent Spring," "For Instance," and "Those Who Want Out," by Denise Levertov. Reprinted by permission of New Directions Publishing Corp.

"Tasting the Land" by Jarold Ramsey from his *Hand Shadows*. Copyright ©1989. Reprinted by permission of Jarold Ramsey.

Library of Congress Cataloging-in-Publication Data
Poetry from the Amicus journal / introduction by Brian Swann ;
    designed and illustrated by Andrea Hendrick.
            p.    cm.
      ISBN 0-935382-76-3
      1. Nature—Poetry.     2. Environmental protection—Poetry.
    3. American poetry—20th century.    I. The Amicus journal.
    PS595.N22P64     1990
    811' .5408036—dc20                              90-46315
                                                       CIP

*Printed on recycled paper by Thomson-Shore, Inc., Dexter Michigan*

# TABLE OF CONTENTS

# INTRODUCTION

Some years ago I was asked to take part in a mail forum. The question was, "Why poems, and why in *College English?*" Now, if *College English*, the literary organ of those who have chosen to profess and teach literature, felt it had good reason to ask such a question, how much more reason might *The Amicus Journal* have had? It is, after all, the journal of an organization whose activities are largely legal and scientific. In fact, however, the presence of poetry in its pages has never been an issue. It seems to have been a given. From the start, even before he asked me to become poetry editor, Peter Borrelli, the editor of *Amicus*, had assumed that poetry was part of the process, part of the solution. From the beginning, the magazine has been committed to publishing the best poetry "rooted in nature" that could be obtained by direct solicitation or selected from the growing mail pile.

Many poets today are taking up again their ancient vatic role, becoming, in their own ways, Shelley's "unacknowledged legislators of the world." We are living in a time of retreat for the Platonic demands that we think in isolated mental entities, or adopt a positivistic stance when explaining experience. The myth makers Plato banished have quietly returned. Science itself has become metaphoric and mythic again, witness the wonderful worlds of quantum physics and fractals. The scientific approach is being seen in terms of the beautiful and mysterious, grounded in pleasure.

John Elder writes that attentiveness to nature distinguishes today's American poetry, and that much of this poetry has "come to resemble Hebrew prophesy in its quality of alienated authority" (*Imagining the Earth: Poetry and the Vision of Nature*, 1985). But rather than "a solitary voice from the mountains" calling for renewal, I hear something like a growing choir, part jeremiad, part paean. I prefer to think of the poets Elder discusses so well (some of whom are in our collection) as pointing the way out of the wasteland. As Elder notes, the poets move toward reintegration through transformation, toward a new wholeness ("whole" and "health" are etymologically very close). The poets are rediscovering ancient truths that have been there all along, within the variety of our own spiritual and intellectual traditions. These truths reside still in the Native American tradition, in the Buddhist (particularly in the Zen branch), in the Christian mystical tradition (especially with St. Francis), and in the Jewish (the sixteenth-century Kabbalist Isaac Luria noted how everything, even an "inanimate" object, has a soul). In the nineteenth century, the Romantic Movement kept alive these nondualistic, antimaterialistic traditions. The poets in our anthology are the movement's direct heirs.

So poetry once more has a great and noble argument, as ambitious as Milton's; if not "to justify the ways of God to Man," then to recall mankind to its proper place in nature, in the cosmos, an enterprise as ambitious and eschatological as Milton's.

Part of this great task is to ground human culture in nonhuman reality, with the end, perhaps, of showing the impossibility of making such a distinction. For it is nature that generates myths; it is our psychic raw material. The nonhuman gives the human material and plot. The human returns the impulse; each shapes the other in an active involvement. Yeats said that "man can embody truth, but he cannot know it." Knowing implies separation and distance. Embodiment is the way the soul/self builds. It is the way the poet, the maker, works.

Poets revivify a world that was never dead, though we have done our best to pretend it was—have done our best to make sure it was. Poets refamiliarize and defamiliarize at the same time, with the aim of revelation (though what was being revealed was there all the time). They show the rightness of the world in the rightness of the word. They show how to live attentively; a religious attitude. They let in the "other," and find integration and interdependency, not fear, forerunner of domination. They water ancient roots on which our existence has always depended, though we have realized this only at the last moment, when it might be too late; paleolithic roots, such as the familial relation of man and beast (which had been relegated to the nursery), and our relation to the vegetable world—knowledge that had been transmitted in poetry by Ovid and moralized away by the Middle Ages. (Recently I was glad to see botanists catching up with Ovid. A *New York Times* headline read "Component of Blood Also Found in Plants." The component was hemoglobin.)

In Indo-European, *dhghem* means "earth." It gives us "humus" and "human." "Adam" is from the Hebrew *adamah*, "earth." The poets in this volume, and many other poets who have not yet graced the pages of *Amicus*, return us to the earth, in our full humanity. They locate ultimate reality in the here and now (which is also the there and then), and in the locating is a call for action, even if no more (or no less) than Pound's:

> Do not move
> Let the wind speak
> That is paradise
> (Canto CXX)

Their voices are given by nature, and they give voice to nature, in the sacred principle of reciprocity. Theirs is a very ancient and a very modern utterance. "That which was lost is found," we read in *The Winter's Tale*, that great drama of reconciliation and rebirth. The process of rebirth is painful—the roots of Eliot's "dissociation of sensibility" go back further than he knew.

But this should be a time and occasion for hope and optimism, as we all respond to the greatest challenge mankind has yet to face: survival itself. The "real" will once more have to be made "sacred," something W.H. Auden did not think possible in 1956 when he wrote, in the introduction to John Ashbery's *Some Trees*, that "the poet is perhaps the only kind of person who can say honestly, and knowing what he means, that he would rather have been born in an earlier age than the present. At a time when real men spoke in poetry. When the real was sacred; when people were real when impersonating a god. Real events, sacred events. . . ." Well, if he had traveled, say, to the pueblos, he would have seen people who were real impersonating a god, as they had done for ages. And if he were alive today, he would hear real men and women speaking in poetry that is trying to make the real sacred and the sacred real, seeing life steady and seeing it whole. For this is a new beginning. The poets in this collection (which is only a *selection* from *Amicus*'s first decade, 1979-1989), represent a true and growing avant-garde. But enough! As the good Franciscan Brother Giles exclaimed some centuries ago: *"Bo, bo, molto dico e poco fo!"* ("Blah, blah, lots of yacking, little action!") This poetry, like the Natural Resources Defense Council, our parent organization, is about *action*!

Brian Swann
New York City
1 January 1990

# PHILIP APPLEMAN

## LAST-MINUTE MESSAGE
## FOR A TIME CAPSULE

I have to tell you this, whoever you are:
that on one summer morning here, the ocean
pounded in on tumbledown breakers,
and the north wind, bustling at our door,
whipped the froth into little rainbows,
and a reckless gull swept down the beach
as if to fly were everything it needed,
and I thought of you in your skirring saucers,
looking for clues, and I wanted to write this down,
so it wouldn't be lost forever,
that once upon a time we had
green fields here, and astonishing things,
swans and rabbits and luna moths
and seas that could dazzle your heart with blue shimmer.
And we could have had them still
and welcomed you to Earth, but
we also had the righteous ones
who worshipped the True Faith, and Holy War.
When you go home to your shining galaxy,
say that what you learned
from this dark and barren place is
to beware the righteous ones.

# CHARLES ATKINSON

## "GREEN LIGHT FOR THE MX MISSILE"
*—San Francisco Chronicle*

I've seen owls here—Great Horned;
no owls today. Seen coyotes foraging;
no coyotes either. And small coast deer;
no deer. Just redwoods' dark verticals
staking the field's edge, a seawind
and a slight-green bush shivering knee-high,
sailing a spiderweb with no owner.
Somewhere, something burning.

The usual web: concentric prisms, thinner
radii, almost invisible—all puffed out
in the wind. Purple-gold runs out a strand.
Irregularities mar the web, and tears.
An Irishwoman studied their tensile strength
for five years and learned the guy-strands
are seven times as strong as the web.
Knowledge is power—or about to be.

The sun's crept its path across my hands
and they're cool again—first right, then left.
I'm sorry I haven't learned more birdcalls.
I could start again closer to earth,
where a ground squirrel severed a plantain stem,
took the seedhead in its forepaws
and gnawed it down to crumbs. When I stood up
it spun and disappeared, swishing the weeds.

And a whole field of plantain—
all the way to the crest, plantain bobbing!
I never noticed that tenacious weed . . .
O, it begins this way without fail,
pure passion to know the thing itself—
until the knowledge taken
turns on us at last, raining down
passion at its purest—burning, burning.

# JIM BARNES

## WINTER'S END

*"These sudden ends of time must give us pause.*
*We fray into the future . . .*
                    —Richard Wilbur, *"Year's End"*

Late today the storm clouds come rolling in,
and night is down upon us with a poison
wind. We draw our breaths carefully in, and on
the late winter streets the traffic slows in
obedience to the wind. Children abed
forget their dreams of snow and Christmas sled.

Now is the time their nights are full of flags
atop flowing tents and kites hawking air
rushed from the proverbial northern lair
where the ice folk dance their last jittery jags
before the circuses of southern wind come
to finally drive all glacial gremlins home.

There was a force in winds of yesterday
that we have all but lost. The fateful breeze
for Homer's Greeks brought fame or pregnancies.
In Taos, wind was woman, the Tewas say,
a mean witch of the north and rheumatism.
In Japan, Susanowo sprang from the chasm

of Izanagi's nose: this breath of death
Izanama's spouse sneezed himself free of,
this wind all laden ships ply to lee of,
fleeing the brunt of its immeasurable breadth.
Now the final force of winter's wind wheels
across the roily sky, and thunder peals

like the fiery chariots out of Ezekiel.
Myths such as these indeed do give us cause
to praise first birds headed north. The equinox,
advent of spring, warms us, then makes us feel
heroic: we've fully known our own wrapped worth
in winter's wind, our place in wind on earth.

# MARVIN BELL

## THE STONES

One night in my room
many stones brought together over the years,
each bearing the gouges and pinpricks
of sea and shore life,
and each weighted according to the sea
which first chisels a slate
and then washes it and later writes on it
with an eraser—
these stones, large and small, flat,
rounded, conical, shapely or rough-hewn,
discussed their origins,
and then got around to me. One of them,
the white one full of holes
that wipes off on your hands, said
that he thinks I carry much sadness,
the weight of a heart full of stones,
and that I bring back these others
so that I might live among the obvious
heaviness of the world.
But another said that I carried him
six months in Spain
in a pants pocket and lifted him out
each night to place on the dresser,
and although he is small and flat,
like a planet seen from the moon,
I often held him up to the light,
and this is because I am able to lift
the earth itself. And isn't this
happiness? But a third stone spoke
from where it stood atop papers
and accused me of trying to manage
the entire world, which for the most part
is neither myself nor not myself,
and is also the air around the rim
of a moving wheel, the space beyond Space,
the water within water,
and the weight within the stone.
Then they all asked what right had I
to be happy or unhappy,
when the language of stones
was no different
from the language of a white lump of dung
among the excellent vegetables.

4

# WENDELL BERRY

## THE REASSURER

A people in the throes of national prosperity, who
    breathe poisoned air, drink poisoned water, eat
    poisoned food,
who take poisoned medicines to heal them of the poisons
    that they breathe, drink, and eat,
such a people crave the further poison of official
    reassurance. It is not logical,
but it is understandable, perhaps, that they adore
    their President who tells them that all is well,
    all is better than ever.
The President reassures the farmer and his wife who
    have exhausted their farm to pay for it, and have
    exhausted themselves to pay for it,
and have not paid for it, and have gone bankrupt for
    the sake of the free market, foreign trade, and the
    prosperity of corporations;
he consoles the Navahos, who have been exiled from their
    place of exile, because that poor land contained
    something required for the national prosperity,
    after all;
he consoles the young woman dying of cancer caused by a
    substance used in the normal course of national
    prosperity to make red apples redder;
he consoles the couple in the Kentucky coalfields, who
    sit watching TV in their mobile home on the mud of
    the floor of a mined-out stripmine;
from his smile they understand that the fortunate have
    a right to their fortunes, that the unfortunate have
    a right to their misfortunes, and that these are
    equal rights.
The President smiles with the disarming smile of a man
    who has seen God, and found Him a true American,
    not overbearingly smart.
The President reassures the Chairman of the Board of the
    Humane Health for Profit Corporation of America,
    who knows in his replaceable heart that health, if
    it came, would bring financial ruin;
he reassures the Chairman of the Board of the Victory
    and Honor for Profit Corporation of America, who
    has been wakened in the night by a dream of the
    calamity of peace.

5

# SALLIE BINGHAM

## SNOW ON THE COAL

February: the barges from upstream are white-tipped,
Their coal heaps frozen. The radar turns
Slow as a spring leaf in the blizzard. In the pilot house,
The lethargic pilot is dreaming of his warm bed.
This civilized procession down the Ohio River
Has bleached the blood out of the coal, bleached out
The pain and fear of the boy crushed in the space
Between the conveyor belt and the roof of the seam:
Six inches. They pried him out, scraped him off,
Dumped him in a body bag and sent him home.

As the coal bears no trace of his blood, the dozing pilot
Is wiped clean as a slate of the history of his cargo
Or of his country; the rippled snow-stung river
Has taken care of that. Heavy diesel fumes,
Heavy vibrations of the motor have lulled him
Into a long sleep. He will never wake. His cargo
With its snow veil will arrive at the mouth of the river
Where history begins, with its iron repetitions.

# SUBDIVISION

The man who does not care for trees
cannot care for women.
He tears us like fingers from the ground—
we grasp the red clay as we fall,
tumbling limb over limb
into the gulley

where we lie prostrate
who once wore the sky.

Now the rains will wash us
in the color of blood
as the hill we held slides
into the ravine,
stripped of creeper and crabgrass,
the thin blue of periwinkle,
the early onions.

The man who looks on this destruction
and sees cellar hole, cement block, transom,
looks on a woman and sees wristbone, wishbone,
the pulmonary cavity.

# OHIO RIVER WINTER

The duck hunters are out these winter mornings,
dressed in the uniforms of forgotten armies.
They patrol the river in pairs. The flat wake
of their deeply camouflaged boat hardly marks the water.
They crouch beneath fur-trimmed hoods, their shotguns
laid on their laps, muzzle out. The habit of violence
is as common as the habit of hunger, but
these ducks are too small.
Their bodies, on china plates, do not cover
the painted pink cabbage rose.

# PETER BLUE CLOUD

## A FALLEN OAK

the great, gnarled fingers of roots
have torn free of the granite base,
protector of bedrock mortars
now exposed,
        See, the old
fallen one seems to say,
before my birth there
were a people here
who ground the seedlings
of my ancestors for food
    back then
so long ago when there
was the giving of shade
and the praise and wonder
to saplings.
        Now,
cut me up and
heat the life of your house
and think of me
in warm dreaming,
then spread my ashes thin
beneath my offspring.
   Yes,
there were a people here
    once,
       and if ever
you should meet them
tell them
that I waited
        a long time.

# PHILIP BOOTH

## A LIFE

As quick as a hawk's wing tipped
to miss my windshield,
                                I heard myself
swerve my cry
                        as she sideslipped into
a hardwood grove:
                            six years now:
                                                her wings
still lift and touch me as
she sails all the way through.

# PETER BORRELLI

## THE RIVER

The river, cold and dark as gun metal,
white streamers advancing,
rushes the gabions and riprap
of the near shore.

Sailboats tug and recoil
at their moorings, their halyards
and shackles jangling in the wind.

Willows sway over the embankment,
their long leaves raking the water.

In the sheltered cove a night heron
feeding among the reeds and hyacinth
senses the coming violence and pauses.

Its ruby eye meets mine
with neither fear nor sympathy.
We are not one
but captured in the same moment.

## TO JOHN MUIR

Across the valley, blue hills.
Above, the river's haze.
A red-tailed hawk turns slowly.
Rooftops in the village
Cluster among the trees.
A crazy-quilt spreads
Over the Pleistocene wake.
I lie down
Upon a sun-soaked rock
And each corpuscle of me
Ruttishly absorbs its warmth.
Drawn down to the earth,
Temporarily fossilized,
I am part of all time
And a geography called hope.

# FRED CHAPPELL

## TOLSTOY'S BEAR

*Disgusting Russia,* he told his diary,
*Russia is abysmal;* set down new Rules
Of Life: *Avoid the gaming table, rise early.*
Ben Franklin remained his adorable saint.
Eager and restless, he hung up his sword
And St. Anne's medal. *A thousand vanities . . .*

And saddled the famous horse that made him weep,
Gathered the glossy hounds, and sped to the forest
To make his presence known to the towering bear
Who mauled him promptly. His rifle had missed fire.
Then: Hugger-mugger in the autumn ferns
The monsters embraced for love of the fury of life.
The beaters could not say who was the man
In the cozy tumult. The bear hung on for madness,
The Count was given "a vision of crisp blue sky
Framed sharply by the bright green tossing treetops."
This vision almost cost the man his eye;
He found it in the bear's wounded open mouth.

It was a peasant with his cudgel drove off
The bear galumphing like a creditor
Into the woods. Tolstoy rose and vowed
A better life, newer theories, newer Rules.

Four days later he returned to kill this bear,
And got it skinned and spread on the study floor
Where he could keep a soulful eye upon it;
Marched barefoot up and down, writing his novels.

An early winter descended like silver blindness
Where the Count pawed over his Russian cruelties.

# ALFRED CORN

## DUCK PAIR

Silver water not the standard
late October chill
(and they unmindful,
lost in thought) brings first
our Doctor Mallard dressed in black
and umber, white collar, green silk cap;
his co-stroller of the river
overalled in novitiate brown
cassock, attentive, lending
her invisible ear
to Aquinas being rehearsed,
and why *aqua qua aqua* calls
for measured splashings in the element,
waterwheeling in silver unison,
wherever flowing discourse takes them,
a direct, from down, chin-tucked-under gaze
no small part of their safe-conduct—habits
by now a fact like plumage, axiomatic.

## WINTERGREEN

Least ever evergreen,
forethoughtless wintergreen,
see here! a snowlit pleinair Xmas.
Then who let rain from the red candle
droplets of berries fire-engine red
—scentless as snow, oh, unlike
the leaves that crushed breathe
a green (*gloria deo*),
degree zero Celsius
apple-fresh, mint-angelica flame?

# JOHN DANIEL

## RETURN

*What is this joy? That no animal*
*falters, but knows what it must do?*
— Denise Levertov

When at one in the morning a raccoon
rustles out of the brush
and rises on hind legs peering
like a bear at my lamplit window,
swaying slightly, forelegs out-thrust,
then drops and walks its lumbering walk
into darkness, for a moment
I am wholer than before—
as if joined with the self
I am always losing, who is curious
and curiously sure, who embraces
all things in a calm regard,
never troubles itself
with forethought of death, and always
in the black light of darkness
sees its slow-stepping way.

# JEANNINE DOBBS

## WALK IN WINTER

Walking over the crest of Naticook Hill
I pause in the pool of glass at the roadside
to look across the valley of the Souhegan
to the hills that rise between here and Concord
Then I look halfway down the hill
where my red house goes off in all directions,
thin smoke rising from its chimney

I reflect again on this unremarkable place
where so many have been born and died
leaving these stone walls
and the markers in Meeting House Cemetery
and I reflect on those who left
only the names of these rivers, these hills

The wind strikes and I hurry on down,
my breath coming fast and small,
as if I have suffered a great loss or blessing

# GENE FRUMKIN

## THE SECOND DEATH OF CHACO CANYON

One sickly civilization
guts another of its death,
would rob the valley—
"streaked with rose and ocher
and with green too pale to be quite real"—
of its immaculate ruin.

To save their last strength
our own people flay the past
as if only a bleached sun
rising over an ashen landscape
could water their lives.
The Anasazi, before they fell away

from our history, survived
in the earth's very structure—
their amazing stonework, Pueblo Bonita
with its 650 rooms.
How many lives depended on kiva smoke
to build this honeycomb house?

Now we strip down, with dutiful dreams,
to the black lungs that breathe
coal's desperate energy.
We do not structure earth.
We darken our skies with life
and leave no room for ancient weather.

But who will blame us, after all,
for our loss of this canyon's
godly dimension? If our time
continues so dimly, the books will say
that Chaco was a myth,
that only the ore sustained us.

# THE GAME REFUGE

A passage, this game refuge
near the center of a city growing
out of the sand. The fowl
are safe by this pond
near a great river. If we humans
could glide so silently
in our atmosphere, lift off
but not fly too far from our lives.
If we could see ahead
only to the next bracken-covered bank
and feel in our blood an endless
return to home.
        No, the city grows
around us, the air dimming
with worn light. Heavier, this air,
weighted down by the fuel
that keeps us traveling on
and back, swift migrations
within defined parameters. The more we go
the further we incite a thoughtless need
to harry ourselves. To ask
of our own deadliness a refuge,
survival.
        Green, abundant life
and feathered life. Mallard and duck,
ibis and the visiting geese
from Canada. Squirrels storing
their winter away. Bees thorough and full
in their buzzing.
        A man comes
to look, to get away from his destiny
for an hour. He is distracted
by money and love. He is aware
of his death. Outside his mind
the city burns on from road to road:
another shape of wild life,
endangered. And he with it,
he in great numbers looks for
water, the lotus and red osiers,
somewhere set aside for use in passage,
time reset short of death,
that first thought edging to the shore.

# BRENDAN GALVIN

## POEM OF THE TOWHEE

Peripheral leaf-shufflers,
they're a black stroke of
the Japanese brush
over a reddish, quietly
passionate streak.
This one has bunted the window
all spring, baffled by glass,
and now, over my head,
a gray, humped spider has set up
like a text creeper
before the poem the towhee
printed there in accents
grave and acute, in characters
beyond any translation.

# XU GANG

## THE NORTHERN MOUNTAIN

Now there's a mountain to remember!
Nothing pretty or magnificent
But simple as yellow loess.
The blame it has taken for ferociousness
Goes as far back as time.

I lean upon a chaotic heap of stones.
My heart is so close to them
That it feels their warmth.
No words here, just an expanse of waving grass
Blown by winds from the empty valley.
I have picked out a fragment that history lost.

This, the Northern Mountain, once had
Splendid peaks and ridges too sublime for words.
Flowers, trees, and songbirds used to thrive there;
So did a clear spring that people said was holy.
Incense smoke curled up inside a Buddhist temple.

The forest has plenty of axes and clubs,
The loggers' rudeness enshrouds the mountain.
Tall trees and short ones
Fall down one after another.
Having lost this protective screen,
The low grass and the wellspring
Die away in grief.

Why not chase away the axes and clubs?
Since ancient times, we have found it hardest
To deprive ourselves of cutting tools
And reasons for cutting.
"When there shall be no more tree cutting"—
That is the green fantasy of the deserted mountain,
A dream so long and simple . . .

*Translated by Dennis Ding and Edward Morin*

# ALBERT GOLDBARTH

## HISTORY AS HORSE LIGHT

It ended at the time of Hiroshima. Everything
ended, the world. Though some of us didn't
know it, and kept on, like the spasms you see
in the hips of an animal—small and useless
telegraph keys—where it's stretched at the edge of the road.
But it wasn't that slow for the horse
at Hiroshima: they'll show you its shadow
burnt permanently to a wall by the blast.
Think of such light. In *Guernica*, Picasso approaches light
like that—flash—a whole horse screaming.

*

It began in the Paleolithic caves. Something,
someone, surely happened before that, but
whatever matters took its first idea
of its shape in those blindblack passageways.
Somebody crawled, with a raw lamp, with a wick
and its fat. Somebody made his way through
rockgut, crawling on his knees like a beast,
rising where the space permitted, making his necessary
Aurignacian way to a place where a horse could be put
on a wall in the first light's first distinctions.

*

And between those two . . . It all went on, we
tried, on some days we relaxed from trying, and then
we'd try again. I pulled off the highway. Siesta
Motel, with a green neon stallion. Its head kept
jerking out of sleep then dropping back in. What
was I then except a man halfway between
two places, naked and with the bedside light
turned off? And what was I *then*, but a retinal plate
discharging its sparks for the day? A skillet sputtering
brilliant greases, pure and imageless, down the dark.

# PATRICK WORTH GRAY

## PHOTOGRAPH

Arnett, Oklahoma, from Wesley Bishop's Back porch—
a huge nightmare made of the Great Plains,
Or that neck just northwest of the Washitas.
A pickup truck here and there, not one
Within sight of the next, as though they are driven
From one oasis to another; no highway
Visible, lolling like a blacksnake. A dumb war
Bristles the brooms in the beds of the pickups,
Sharpens the outlines of the roofs, this wide glimpse
Of the prairie and not a cowboy in view.
And not a sign of Custer, or Black Kettle,
The brown women's hands trampled by cavalry,
Teepees burned along the Little Robe. So much
Is missing: the buff-brick bank, the new high school,
Yucca around the orange water tower.
There must be a reason he has snapped
The west horizon, its sifted grit of poverty.

On the horizon, past the last pickup truck,
A tavern, its windows walleyed, hunkers down
Below Black Mesa, waiting for closing time—
One of the few oases in this desert.
Atop the mesa, antelope taste the breeze,
Whiff the stench of man, their antlers fragile
Against the end of sky. The picture cannot hope
To show the antelope trot away to graze
On redroot and nimblewill far past the smash
Of fist on flesh rolling in the dandelions.
And Marion, gaping in his lawnchair, huge,
Crocheting, and crying for his mother,
He remembers a night like this—quiet father
Cleaning, oiling, blueing the gun for mother,
And her nodding over pictures of daughters

Long since gone. If he had seen Wesley Bishop
Focus on the Longhorn Saloon, aim his lens
At that aim of the .30-.30, would he
Mourn now with great yawps and cases of Lone Star
Father and mother in this final dust, drool
His name to the men who stagger to their trucks,
Remind them of the reason they must go home?

# JOHN HAINES

## ANCESTOR OF THE HUNTING HEART

*—after Breugel*

There is a distance in the heart,
and I know it well—
leaf-somberness of winter branches,
dry stubble scarred with frost,
late of the sunburnt field.

Neither field, nor furrow,
nor woodlot patched with fences,
but something wilder: a distance
never cropped or plowed,
only by fire and the blade of the wind.

The distance is closer than
the broomswept hearth—
that time of year when leaves
cling to the bootsole,
are tracked indoors,
lie yellow on the kitchen floor.

Snow is a part of the distance,
cold ponds, and ice
that rings the cattle-trough.

Trees that are black at morning
are in the evening grey.
The distance lies between them,
a seed-strewn whiteness
through which the hunter comes.

Before him in the ashen snow-litter
of the village street
an old man makes his way,
bowed with sack and stick.

A child is pulling a sled.

The rest are camped indoors,
their damped fires smoking
in the early dusk.

## FOREST WITHOUT LEAVES

This earth written over with words,
with names, and the names
come out of the ground,
the words like spoken seeds.

What field, what dust,
what namesake for a stone
that moves by inches
and clears a path in the mud?

Ice moved once, a river of stones,
and the road it drove
through the forest can still be walked.
Look there, you will find
for your house a standing boulder.

Earth worn deep by its names,
written over with words:

there are spaces inside those words
and silence for the clearing
where no house stands.

# DONALD HALL

## SURFACE

The surveyor climbs a stonewall into woods
scribbled with ferns, saplings, and dead oaktrees

where weltering lines trope themselves into stacks
of vegetation. He sees an ash forced around a rock

with roots that clutch on granite like a fist
grasping a paperweight. He stares at hemlocks

rising among three-hundred-year-old sugarmaples
that hoist a green archive of crowns: kingdom

of fecund death and pitiless survival. He observes
how birch knocked down by wind and popple chewed

by beaver twist over and under each other, branches
abrasive when new-fallen, turning mossy and damp

as they erase themselves into humus, becoming
polyseeded earth that loosens with lively pokeholes

of creatures that watch him back: possum, otter,
fox. Here the surveyor tries making his mark:

He slashes a young oak; he constructs a stone
cairn at a conceptual right-angle; he stamps

his name and the day's date onto metal tacked
to a stake. His text established, he departs

the life-and-death woods, where cellular life keeps
pressing upward from underground offices to read

sun and study slogans of dirt: "Never consider
a surface except as the extension of a volume."

# JIM HARRISON

## THE IDEA OF BALANCE IS TO BE FOUND IN HERONS AND LOONS

I just heard a loon call on a t.v. ad
and my body gave itself
a quite voluntary shudder,
as in the night in East Africa
I heard the immense barking cough
of a lion, so foreign and indifferent.

But the lion drifts away
and the loon stays close,
calling as she did in my childhood,
in the cold rain a song
that tells the world of men
to keep its distance.

It isn't the signal of another life
or the reminder of anything
except her call: still,
at this quiet point past midnight
the rain is the same rain
that fell so long ago, and the loon
says I'm seven years old again.

*At the far ends of the lake*
*where no one lives or visits—*
*there are no roads to get there;*
*you take the watercourse way,*
*the quiet drip and drizzle*
*of oars, slight squeak of oarlock,*
*the bare feet can feel the cold water*
*move beneath the old wood boat.*

At one end the lordly, great blue herons
nest at the top of the white pine;
at the other end the loons,
just after daylight in cream-colored mist,
drifting with wails that begin as querulous,
rising then into the spheres in volume,
with lost or doomed angels imprisoned
within their breasts.

# JANE HIRSHFIELD

## IN SMOOTH WATER THE MOUNTAINS SUSPEND THEMSELVES

Here, where shallows and hillside
echo each other
so perfectly, who is to say
what is water, what sky,
or what perfection it is that arches
a squirrel's grey body
from oak tree to pine, thirty feet in the air?
He does not think of himself
as one of the many possible angels
plucked from the blue of this lake,
as the one that chose to manifest, just now.
To him, it is no surprise when he crosses
the dim, suspended fluttering of a fish
mid-way in his climb
up the vertical trunk of the world.
He is like one of those ancient creatures
found on cathedral walls,
lion-mouthed, vulture-clawed, with bulging eyes—
how calmly they survey the doors and windows,
what enters, what departs.
No human passage concerns them,
compared to the cool weight of stone,
to the beings whose size those enormous openings fit;
and we, in turn, barely glance towards
their bodied faith sluiced over with rain,
bearded in ice, as we pass beneath.
So the wind-roughened fur of the squirrel brushes
against the belly of the big brown
and their doubles,
perfectly camouflaged above, below,
know nothing of that meeting, its cold, quick touch.
And we, who quarry the earth for silver and granite
with any step,
do not feel the green clouds of treetops, green clouds of weeds—
how they rest like folded wings in the clear water,
patient, waiting, having borne us this far.

# BEN HOWARD

## BRINK

After the cold
light of March
the first leaves
of the crabapple
open, the cherry's
branches thicken.
Another winter
dwindles as if
it had never begun.

The scars stay:
broken shale,
the split plank.
All day one waits
for certainties,
as though the wear
of eave and trough,
cheek and hand,
might be forestalled:
as though this sense
of falling forward,
helpless and cold,
were but a sly
illusion. Rich

in loss, replete
with winter's bitterness,
the earth receives
our misplaced hope
and vain desire.
Look: new growth
on the yew, new color
nurtured in damp remains.

# MISSISSIPPI SNAPPERS

They were better left uncaught. They came
Out of the river in dripping traps,
Their armor muddy, their lizard-heads
Covered with slime. All they could do

Was harm. And when they lunged at us
Through the wet ropes, we saw no fright
But only virulence in their eye-slits,
Spite and defiance in their eyes.

Were we their jurors or their kin
In hiding? Taking them home, we saw
Our inmost quarrels in the jaws
That fought our sticks, the hearts that beat

After dismemberment, the shells
Hung up like shields on the market's walls.

# DAVID IGNATOW

## DUSK

In the gathering dark, the tree trunk bare
in the wintry scene outside my window
resembles a gigantic aorta, its branches
spread in all directions
to feed the sky its life,
earth the body, and I on that body
being fed the sky.

## A LEAF

A leaf is spiralling directly at the tall grass
without wavering or hesitation, as if knowing
in advance where it must go. And now it lies
hidden in the grass, not stirring, content
with itself, I would say, having left the tree
to find itself a place on earth.

## THIS MORNING

I've spent this morning studying the leaves
in the wind and have concluded they prefer
to remain still to dwell upon themselves
in quiet. They settle back upon their branches
in the absence of wind and are composed.

I've also studied the wind
and have concluded it prefers its own ways
to stillness and order. Every now and then
it charges through the leaves
and shakes them up, as if to remind them.

# GEORGE KEITHLEY

## WHEN THEY LEAVE

When they leave the world will be at peace
forever. A room with wide windows
shut against the weather. Wind
beyond the glass bending the brilliant maples.
Will we hear wings beating out of those trees?

Who can inhabit the unholy sleep
of the soul once they wander
silently away? Who'll bark, howl,
bray, croak, whirr, whinny, all
together raise their joyful noise? None

of these creatures who breed and birth
their young and feed
so near to us
a man forgets
the grace granted to each one—

Cattle
because they are convenient—

Coyotes
because they are not—

The cats
which remind us of our debts—

The sentimental dog who swallows his pride
and happily prevails
by licking plates.

Ordinary horses
who carry their ancient hearts under ours.

Also the bristling hog we hate and eat.

The customary spotted goat we know
will never acknowledge its guilt—

Black clouds of crows who strut
among the muddy furrows
at seedtime. Hosts of locusts
floating like smoke over the fields—
The brown bats in love with our streetlamps.

Droves of animals who mate and thrive
and swarm before our eyes only
to disappear when we dream
because they are too innocent
to survive.

# MAXINE KUMIN

## HOMAGE TO BINSEY POPLARS

*O if we but knew what we do when*
*we delve or hew*   —G.M. Hopkins

The arctic fox of Kiska now is quelled
not spared, not one that preyed upon the goose
the rare Aleutian goose, all, all are felled—

Our only white fox (in the winter phase)
swept from the island for the goose's sake
by poison pellets scattered on the ice—

the small endangered goose around whose neck
a narrow ring of white may grow no more
unless the purge of foxes lures it back.

The fox that Russian traders brought ashore
in 1836 to multiply
thence to be harvested year after year

hung leanly on in Kiska till the sly
and fecund Norway rat with nearly nak-
ed tail arrived, shipborne by the Allies.

The rat that fed on garbage stayed to suck
the yolks from eggs, untidy omnivore.
Fox banqueted on goose but kept in check

the Old World rat that bids now to devour
each wished-for clutch on Kiska, to the rue
of federal Fish and Wildlife officers

who, sizing up the prospects of the few
in saving one, eradicated two.

# SYDNEY LEA

## UNEXAMPLED FEAR

Black thieves, red-tailed darters . . .
All the kingbird's foes
know that he wants no heart.
Whatever it means, I also
know his courage. My better
self salutes him, springing
against his bullies, or when
I hear him singing,
to call it that. His fan
is a flag of white surrender's
opposite. My better
self may resist the softer
way some sun-filled day.

A blaze of lichen beads.
Devil's Paintbrush. Aster.
Blackberry flowers' beige.
A nap of Queen Anne's Lace.
Here are the sidehill pastures
eager for morning, gorged
on years away from the plough,
dull leveler. I've urged
myself to the upper meadow
at dawn. The small breasts torn,
three kingbird chicks, dead,
lie at height of land.

The hen in a thorn
above them cocks her head
bold to sky. Down figures
among the hardhack stands
and night-soaked stalks of milkweed
threaded together by spiders.
The day will fair, the sun
will light the understory:
rodents' constellations
of tunnels, dark strawberries—
enough to stoop to, pluck
and stuff into my shirt.
There's a tiny feather stuck
in the bloodred juice on my finger.

I wipe it off in the dirt.
But like a maudlin stranger
I go on to the vine-choked grave
—what's left of it, a ditch—
of Drooge, poor leveled farmer.
Day breaks like a bird-full wave,
shrill with high hawk and crow.
The berries stain their pouch
above my heart. I turn it
inside out to my mouth
and suck like a madman, burning
with day, its sweetness, woe,
the frank sun burning south.

# DENISE LEVERTOV

## FOR INSTANCE

Often, it's nowhere special: maybe
a train rattling not fast or slow
from Melbourne to Sydney, and the light's fading,
we've passed that wide river remembered
from a tale about boyhood and fatal love, written
in vodka prose, clear and burning—
the light's fading and then
beside the tracks this particular
straggle of eucalyptus, an inconsequential
bit of a wood, a coppice, looks your way,
not at you, through you, through the train,
over it—gazes with branches and rags of bark
to something beyond your passing. It's not,
this shred of seeing, more beautiful
than a million others, less so than many;
you have no past here, no memories,
and you'll never set foot among these shadowy
tentative presences. Perhaps when you've left this continent
you'll never return; but it stays with you:
years later, whenever
its blurry image flicks on in your head,
it wrenches from you the old cry:
O Earth, belovéd Earth!
              —like many another faint
constellation of landscape does, or fragment
of lichened stone, or some old shed
where you took refuge once from pelting rain
in Essex, leaning on wheel or shafts
of a dusty cart, and came out when you heard
a thrush return to song though the rain
was not quite over; and, as you thought there'd be,
there was, in the dark quarter where frowning clouds
were still clustered, a hesitant trace
of rainbow; and across from that the expected
gleam of East Anglian afternoon light, and leaves
dripping and shining. Puddles, and the roadside weeds
washed of their dust. Earth,
that inward cry again—
*Erde, du liebe* . . .

# SILENT SPRING

O, the great sky!

Green and steep
the solid waves of the land,
breasts, shoulders, haunches,
serene.

The waveless ocean
arches its vertical silver,
molten, translucent.

Fine rain
browses the valleys, moves
inland.
And flocks
of sunlight fly
from hill to hill.
The land
smiles in its sleep.

But listen:

no crisp susurration of crickets.
One lone frog. One lone
faraway whippoorwill. Absence.
no hum, no whirr.
And look:

the tigerish thistles, bold
yesterday,
curl in sick yellowing.

Drop the wild lettuce!
Try not to breathe!

Laboriously
the spraytruck
has ground its way
this way.
Hear your own steps
in violent silence.

# THOSE WHO WANT OUT

In their homes, much glass and steel. Their cars
are fast—walking's for children, except in rooms.
When they take longer trips, they think with contempt
of the jet's archaic slowness. Monastic
in dedication to work, they apply honed skills,
impatient of less than perfection. They sleep by day
when the bustle of lives might disturb their research,
and labor beneath fluorescent light in controlled environments
fitting their needs, as the dialects
in which they converse, with each other or with
the machines (which are not called machines)
are controlled and fitting. The air they breathe
is conditioned. Coffee and coke keep them alert.
But no one can say they don't dream,
that they have no vision. Their vision
consumes them, they think all the time
of the city in space, they long for the permanent colony,
not just a lab up there, the whole works,
malls, racquet courts, hot tubs, state-of-the-art
ski machines, entertainment . . . Imagine it, they think,
way out there, outside of "nature," unhampered,
a place contrived by man, supreme
triumph of reason. They know it will happen.
*They do not love the earth.*

# PETER MEINKE

## THE TRASHING OF GATLINBURG

Beauty is momentary in the land
but if you're quick you can cash in on it.
When rivers flow, will fast food lag behind
or Port-o-potties, where the tourists sit?
Americans prefer, de Tocqueville said,
the useful to the beautiful, but if
the beautiful is sold like marmalade
we'll learn to love it, cashing in our strips.

Still, the Little Pigeon River purls
past rhododendron snowing in the woods
cleansing itself, setting an example
we don't follow, changing our Good to goods;
while nature and greed, like lovers, interlock
stretched out in Gatlinburg, with greed on top.

# W.S. MERWIN

## THE INAUGURATION: 1985

We have elected the end
because we have looked on everything alive
with a look that has killed it
and we see it already dead

the moon races
in clouds from the beginning
the earth our victim shines in the moonlight
in the light of the moon our victim

the land is gone there are only numbers
our long conquest has been an explosion
we are flying from the center
multiplying as we burn

# ROGER MITCHELL

## OF WILLIAM STILLMAN
## (1828-1901)

His life lived in the semi-pathetic way
of the post-Romantic man of leisure,
his genius dispersed, ambition blunted,
by too close a glimpse of something,
      which I will get to.

Later, travelled, did jobwork for newspapers,
the government, consul in a few places,
called himself finally a journalist,
who had it in him to paint, and did,
      briefly.

One hangs in the Concord Public Library
which I have seen only in bad reductions,
black and gray, in books, not about him,
but Emerson, who stands mute in the middle of it,
      looking lost and away.

Not that he gave up art. Who wouldn't have then?
Most lit out for Europe at the first chance
or locked themselves up at home, did not come back
or out, the work assuming that flow and stoppage,
      like wrapped feet

among Chinese nobility, a badge of enviable
uselessness. Stillman, though, is useful now,
so far from the nineteenth century and the thing
he saw there which many, even the brightest,
      neglected to mention

or carried like a last meal into the ground,
bits of half-digested organic matter,
we're not sure what, maybe corn meal and water.
I speak of the woods partly,
      partly of something else.

Certainly not that clump at the edge of town
or the next county, where one picnics among barrels
full of aluminum cans, but the thing that vanished
about the same time, and for most of the same reasons
      as the indian.

We have here in Indiana a patch, I have seen it,
of uncut trees, original growth. An acre or two, at best.
People drive for miles just to look at it.
Whole families, if large enough, can hug
        its biggest tree.

It is a zoo to us, a kind of gorilla
brought from another continent, as bananas are brought
to the supermarket, an invisible miracle,
as in stooping to pick up a tossed bottle we forget
        we are stooping.

Stillman went there in '54 and found what he knew
his going there would kill. "This superb solitude,"
Emerson called it in his two-week camp-out four years later
with Agassiz and the rest, each with a guide,
        Stillman the host,

who stayed on after the others left,
sent his guide back to the settlement,
one of the Martins, I think, from Saranac,
and didn't come out till November.
        And nearly not then.

The wilderness dwindles (is gone, really)
under the human needs for it, Stillman
one of the last to feel there, as if by reversion,
the hush of creation, world before man.
        Which is why

this man, an American, at his life's end
tried to make in the blunt soil of Frimley Green, Surrey,
his home of the moment, with cuttings and seeds
sent there from Albany, a thing that was now only
        inside him.

# RUTH MOOSE

## READING TO ROCKS

Some listen, moss ears
alert to sounds and shapes
of words I shout.
They thrive in rooted places,
sit calm as ladies at church.
Their Easter hats are leaves,
velvet and a cardinal netted
in the crown. Others are nervous
as dragon flies in rain. Their
attention runs to other places, ends
in the lake. An old man
in the corner died
a thousand years ago, turned
into a thinking statue.
He is sculpted weather, molded
storm. Most sleep
I hear their dreams.

# DUANE NIATUM

## IMAGINARY DRAWINGS OF THE SONG ANIMALS

I

Treefrog winks without springing
from its elderberry hideaway.
Before the day is buried in dusk
I will trust the crumbling earth.

II

Foghorns, the bleached absence
of the Cascade and Olympic mountains.
The bay sleeps in a shell of haze.
Anchorless as the night,
the blue-winged teal dredges for the moon.

III

Thistle plumed,
a raccoon pillages my garbage.
When did we plug its nose with concrete?
Whose eyes lie embedded in chemicals?

IV

Dams abridge the Columbia Basin.
On the rim of a rotting barrel,
a crow. The impossible remains
of a cedar man's salmon trap.

V

Deer crossing the freeway—
don't graze near us, don't trust our signs.
We hold your ears in our teeth,
your hoofs on our dashboards.

VI

Shells, gravel musings from the deep,
dwellings from the labyrinth of worms.
Crabs crawl sideways into another layer of dark.

VII

Bumblebee,
a husk of winter and the wind.
I will dance in your field
if the void is in bloom.

VIII

A lizard appears, startled by my basket
of blackberries. In the white
of the afternoon we are lost to the stream.
Forty years to unmask the soul!

# JULIA OLDER

## GEORGES BANK

*I have seen them riding seaward on the waves*
*combing the white hair of the waves blown back.*
                                        —T.S. Eliot

I

They were fishing two centuries or more,
the men of Gloucester, when our great grandmothers
stepped off the boats at Ellis Island.
Out the harbor they sailed half asleep,
lantern light snaking through the channel.
They bloodied their new mitts with fish gurry
to protect their hands from the winter's raw chapping
and drew in seines of small fry, flashing
on the first silver veins of morning sun.
The ship-jacks trawled shoals of friendly cod
chaperoned by monsters of the deep—
the hone-toothed wolf and hammer-headed shark,
the rat-faced eel and gum-sucking nurse.
At home their wives sewed pairs of worsted nippers
from old socks and climbed the steep stairs
to the widow's walk, clutching silent children
in a dark labyrinth of windy skirt.
The old Gloucester salts built their clippers
increasing shoal and over-stretched the sail
beyond the bow to reach Georges Bank.
With speed they breeched the jutting Capes
and scudded back before the duskingtide.
On short-lived days black as a miner's cave
they went down with the seductive widow-maker.

## II

Still, before the morning star appears
the steel clad fishing fleet moves out,
an incandescent arc, to Georges Bank.
The two-ton doors descend into the sea,
an open-sesame to rising schools. Depth sounders
trace ascending scales. And now the winch
draws up the dripping purse and lets it plunge,
an avalanche of glitter on the deck.
Their shovels scoop the catch into the hold
and long before it's dusk the fish are sold
to those who never saw the Gloucester light.
The Japanese with wide Minolta eyes
weigh tuna at the wharf and fly it home.
The Continental Shelf sets a buffet
of eel for Holland, inky squid for Spain.
Poultry farmers far from saline water
silo fishmeal on the dusty plain.
Cogs and gears of industry worldwide
are lubricated with a piscene oil,
fine and miscible where crude is not.
Fearless as their grandfathers before them
the men of Gloucester trawl the turgid surf
across the double helix of the Bank
that builds the food chain like a graduated
string of pearls with whose final link
their lives, as ours, irreclaimably are fated.

## CARETTA CARETTA

The loggerhead turtle
swims slowly toward the dunes
where she deposits a hundred
moons wet and white as porcelain
in a black hole.

Raccoon eclipse
who would steal night
scampers across the sand
and bolts down all but one
that hangs luminous and fragile
in a far corner of Cassiopeia.

*The title is the Latin name for the loggerhead turtle.*

# MARY OLIVER

## FIVE A.M. IN THE PINEWOODS

I'd seen
their hoofprints in the deep
needles and knew
they ended the long night

under the pines, walking
like two mute
and beautiful women toward
the deeper woods, so I

got up in the dark and
went there. They came
slowly down the hill
and looked at me sitting under

the blue trees, shyly
they stepped
closer and stared
from under their thick lashes and even

nibbled some damp
tassels of weeds. This
is not a poem about a dream,
though it could be.

This is a poem about the world
that is ours, or could be.
Finally
one of them—I swear it!—

would have come to my arms.
But the other
stamped sharp hoof in the
pine needles like

the tap of sanity,
and they went off together through
the trees. When I woke
I was alone,

I was thinking:
so this is how you swim inward,
so this is how you flow outward,
so this is how you pray.

## PIPEFISH

In the green
   and purple weeds
      called *Zostera*, loosely
         swinging in the shallows,

I waded, I reached
   my hands
      in that most human
         of gestures—to find,

to see,
   to hold whatever it is
      that's there—
         and what came up

wasn't much
   but it glittered
      and struggled,
         it had eyes, and a body

like a wand,
   it had pouting lips.
      No longer,
         all of it,

than any of my fingers,
   it wanted
      away from my strangeness,
         it wanted

to go back
   into that waving forest
      so quick and wet.
         I forget

when this happened,
   how many years ago
      I opened my hands—
         like a promise

I would keep my whole life,
   and have—
      and let it go.
         I tell you this

in case you have yet to wade
   into the green
      and purple shallows
         where the diminutive

pipefish
   wants to go on living.
      I tell you this
         against everything you are—

your human heart,
   your hands passing over the world,
      gathering and closing,
         so dry and slow.

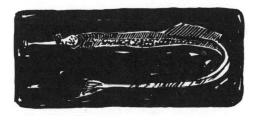

# SPRING

Somewhere
    a black bear
        has just risen from sleep
            and is staring

down the mountain.
    All night
        in the brisk and shallow restlessness
            of early spring

I think of her,
    her four black fists
        flicking the gravel,
            her tongue

like a red fire
    touching the grass,
        the cold water.
            There is only one question:

how to love this world.
    I think of her
        rising
            like a black and leafy ledge

to sharpen her claws against
    the silence
        of the trees.
            Whatever else

my life is
    with its poems
        and its music
            and its glass cities,

it is also this dazzling darkness
    coming
        down the mountain,
            breathing and tasting;

all day I think of her—
    her white teeth,
        her wordlessness,
            her perfect love.

# JOSÉ EMILIO PACHECO

## FIRST DEGREE EQUATION
## WITH ONE VARIABLE

In the city's last river, by mistake
or phantasmagoric incongruence, I suddenly
saw a fish that was almost dead. It gasped
poisoned by the dirty water, lethal
as our air. What a furor
    its round lips
    its mouth's zero in motion.
    Perhaps nothingness
    or the unspeakable word,
    the last voice
    of nature in the valley.
The only salvation for him
was to choose between two forms of asphyxiation.
The double death throes haunt me.
The torture of the water and its inhabitant.
    His pained glance at me,
    his wish to be heard,
    his irrevocable sentence.
I will never know what he tried to tell me,
this voiceless fish that only spoke
the omnipotent language of our mother,
death.

*Translated by Linda Scheer*

# JAROLD RAMSEY

## TASTING THE LAND

*"To become shamans, Lillooet boys were required to bathe
in every lake and stream in their country."*

Wherever water gathers, or pours over stone
in our land, we are sent forth.
The old men, they teach us the spirit
is like the sky, it must have water
to clear itself, and shine.
The spirit, they say, can become a rainbow.
Soon I will have taken the powers
of every lake and river, pond and creek
in our world—already I can taste
my way through most of the land,
the sweet, the brackish, the stagnant,
the salty, the ice-cold.
Through the densest thicket at dusk
I can track my mind to that sudden blue opening
where the sky plunges in to a lake,
and ringed by spruce be bathed again anew.
Someday, though we must go through the country of sand
and bones, or the country of smoke and fire,
and our bodies will stiffen and shrivel, still
our spirits will shine, they say, and dance,
on the far waters of home.

# PAUL ROCHE

## SIZE IS NOT THE SOUL

Size is not the soul
nor is the neutron small
when eyes go beyond the gazing
and gazer beyond his cell

Dust is more than matter
The quantum does not wither
fused in a leaf or a flower
then back where none can gather

Behind its waves of pulsing
the atom is creating . . .
Within beyond behind it
what tremulous drive is thinking?

# NORMAN H. RUSSELL

## THE MESSAGE OF THE RAIN

when i was a child
i was a squirrel a bluejay a fox
and spoke with them in their tongues
climbed their trees dug their dens
and knew the taste
of every grass and stone
the meaning of the sun
the message of the night
now i am old and past
both work and battle
and know no shame
to go alone into the forest
to speak again to squirrel fox and bird
to taste the world
to find the meaning of the wind
the message of the rain.

# REG SANER

## DESERT SPACE

A great garden of blossoming nails
and blue zenith, jet-streaked, and red sandstone
whose sheep bells tinkle across the arroyo.
Their herdsman? You see none.
But because it's our nature never to rest
in the world we've been given
a Navajo pickup flashes past, hurrying
into stillness.
The wood dove flutters beyond the hawk's
patient glide, and your thumb
rubbing dust off a moving Anasazi hand
fire-brightened into glaze
on this potsherd you've stopped for
empties all 800 rooms of ruin famously ancient—
Pueblo Bonito—to your own skull's *tabula rasa*,
giving lessons in how to be, and want to be,
exactly where you are,
which is how you enter the primeval
hush on this land
quiet as a planet in motion,
or the 747, melting away
to a sheep bell.

# AGAIN THE APPLES RIPEN LIKE HILLS

. . . and our October fields dwindle off
into somewhere on the feebler side of this orbit,
signaling distress—international orange, blaze red,
yellows, ochres. When a disconsolate robin
tosses itself off the mesa rim
descending
by low dips and glides over casual slaughters of frost
I take for my cue those breastfeathers
ashen as light in December
and rise up and walk
out from under that sun's winter arches,
packing its least haggard patches of sky
into June, then July, and all of that into August.
Knee deep in memorized scenes, I ascend foothills
swaled with fern, scattering grasshoppers
off weed stalks like grain,
rising high into quillwort, rock aster
and Indian paintbrush, and mosses heavily cleft
by the single-file hoofprints of elk
I seem to be trailing up toward the thick half-acre meadows
whose blossoming aims at three weeks of glory
making all summer,
last summer, my season
for hiking there still, for gathering everything,
parting with nothing.

# TERRENCE SAVOIE

## READING SUNDAY

clouds is 19th century
lying outside in the tall grass
with my hands pillowed behind my head
and thinking how Emily Dickinson
might have done it upstairs
in her bedroom or while walking
home after church services.
Who'ld've guessed?
The way, for instance, John Muir,
when he was only Johnny and tending
sheep for a few months in the high Sierras,
got up a journal with cloud-words in it
like "bossy" and "butter-colored."
Just for fun, I've been watching
the little ones that aren't butter-
colored but angry and sitting
on the edge of the pot of sky like
mongrels exhausted with the rain.

# SUSAN FROMBERG SHAEFFER

## THE VINE

I believe, I said,
In the resurrection of all the dumb things.

All around me
The elephant-skinned elms

Were fluttering their huge green leaves,
Those trees which had stood

All winter long
Like big animals in a boneyard.

The breeze died in the leaves
And the elms held their leaves out,

Flat, big as porches in the hot air.

I see, I said, and make note of it,
The red current in the rose stem.

Perhaps the trick is to sleep deep enough,
Or to close one's eyes before the fall shakes

All the colors loose.
Then I saw the vine.

Grey and dry,
It climbed high as the house.

It looked deader than driftwood,
Than egg cartons, than a jellyfish

In the basin of a desert.
It will come back, I said,

But I did not believe it,
Although, for years, it had come back.

I mourned that vine.
The next week, it was alive.

The wind tossed its leaves like waves.
It waved at me with its many hands.

When I held my hand
Up to the sun,

I saw all the veins' traceries
Like veins in a leaf.

I felt hope.
The sun winked from behind a cloud.

The vine laughed in the little breeze:
Our world,
Not yours.

# GARY SNYDER

## HAIDA GWAI NORTH COAST, NAIKOON BEACH, HIELLEN RIVER RAVEN CROAKS

*Queen Charlotte Islands*

Twelve ravens squawk, squork, crork
Over the dark tall spruce
   and down to the beach.
Two eagles squabbling, twitter, meeting,
Bumping flying overhead

Amber river waters
Dark from muskeg acids, irons,
Murk the stream of tide-wall eagre coming up
Over the sandspit, through the drumming surf,
Eagles, ravens, seagulls, over surf,
Salal and cedar at the swelling river,

   wheeling birds make comment:

On grey skies, big swells, storms,
The end of summer, the fall run—
Humpy salmon waiting off the bar
   and when they start upstream—

Comment
On the flot and jet of sea crud
And the downriver wash of inland
Hard-won forest natural trash
From an older wildness, from a climax lowland,
   virgin system,

Mother
Earth loves to love.
Love hard, playing, fighting,
Rough and rowdy love-rassling
She can take it, she gives it,
Kissed, bruising, laughing—

Up from old growth mossy bottoms
Twa corbies rork and flutter

   the old food
   the new food

Tangled in fall flood streams.

## TREE SONG

Between dirt dark and giddy sky;
Straight, twisted, mountains, mudflats,
Where we bloom,
        limbs that wait and wave,
Noble Silence for a lifetime's talk.

  across the hills the pollen blows
  a cloud of orgies in the boughy air—

Are we our black wet roots
Or do we live by light?
One hand grips, the other makes a sign.
Scanning slope or gully where it soon must lie.

        I lay
This punky mossy gnarled and
Useless scab-barked worm-ate
Seedless wore out loggy body
—with a great crash—
                down.
My secret heartwood no bud ever knew.

# KATHLEEN SPIVACK

## HOLOGRAM

I sit alone in human-woman form
and seek through separateness, to understand
what there is in the perceived landscape
particular enough to understand:

each singular grassblade, the trefoil arrangement
of ivy and clover, the pine tree's needles on the branch
in bunched distinguished patterns, fives and threes,
that, in pine, spruce, and hemlock make the difference

mostly by placement; the unique organization of
cellular patterns so that each part of a tree
is a logo for *tree* and the observing eye,
accustomed to order, puts it together in generalities,

creating designs as it watches, as a rose
becomes a hologram for *rose*,
and music, complex sound waves, models
upon the complex unfolding of those

petalled emotions we call "soul,"
each thought an electromagnetic symbol for "mind,"
and each person, you, for instance,
standing for all of humankind;

and cryptograms upon a page
which immediately become more than alphabet:
*word*, with its mystery, power
to, at one moment, both create and interpret.

It's true, at each moment we are all
thinking everything, everywhere; even a new baby
opening its sentient eyes
and an old woman, far away, shutting hers, dying;

and that cloud reforming over the valley
shaped just like flying horses,
and dissipating, and a giraffe in Africa
stepping delicately among thorn bushes,

and all the miracles, preposterous, of nature.
How do I know what a tree
is thinking? I don't, although the sap
is drawn upward jubilantly

through tubular spaces into tree-dreaming:
leafy extravagances, branches celebrating;
all that wild sky-life streaming
over the shapes that are *world* in its dances.

# WILLIAM STAFFORD

## AT MALHEUR GAME REFUGE

Coyote Butte rinsed by earthlight begins
to loom, a mound against the background of stars.
A simmer of birds grows louder; then geese
honk, spattering water as they take off, their V
forming slowly and finding true north as they go.
It is any day, any year, any century.
It is dawn, and every bird has an opinion.

These are the good years. You can breathe.
It is possible that your attention will discover
a little colored thread that connects everything.
Besides, you have already paid for tomorrow,
and it may not come for you anyway.
This day floods over the earth and splashes
against you. In the sky your way appears: true north.

## THAT LAKE IN THE MOUNTAINS

Never quite quiet, it accepted what came,
and gave it all back. Sand was its treasure:
"Some day all of these rocks will be sand."
In winter it dulled, but in summer it girlishly
played in the shallows. From all sides an owl
tested its auditorium at night. I camped there
a month but left when my hands began
to reach out in the dark. Even yet there's an echo
behind everything that happens. I hark
of an evening when I stand anywhere in the city
and begin to feel my invisible hands.

71

# TOWARD NOW

1.

Back then someone said, "I will tell them a story
that makes their lives a drama. Their days
will shine forth, and every stone they pass
call out, *We do our part, and you
do yours.*" In sun, in rain, the people
carry their picture of the world with them,
and they look at it mornings and evenings to
    remind
how their meaning could link to whatever
    happens.

2.

But others destroyed that story, over
the years: "Where is the good? Rocks
can't talk. People die. They can't come back.
No matter what you gain or who you are
it all disappears." Then people picked up
and dropped things. They crowded each other.
    Nothing
held their interest for long, or counted
in their lives. Their new story was fast but empty,
and in giddy moments it revealed its own untruth
or shuddered into glimpses of forlorn loss.

3.

Meanwhile certain messengers had come into
    town.
They turned their still faces; they stood; they
    walked
beside others and listened carefully. When
    evening
came these quiet ones let their eyes grow
wide to hold whatever story there is —
not the glorious one, the one that can't stand
the true light, and not the opposing story
that pretends to know an emptiness beyond what
    we know —

4.

But this pageant right here, morning, evening,
the strange unfolding of flowers, and their going,
the quiet, sure finding of friends, who
can also disappear or transform themselves
and ourselves. In the center of this greater story
we look around and become whatever we are,
willingly caught up, being part of what is.

## THE BUSH FROM MONGOLIA

This bush with light green leaves
came from Mongolia where
it learned everything about wind.

All day and all night that cold lesson
clawed its firm hands everywhere
over whatever dared live above the ground.

These branches will never reach out
and celebrate the sun; these roots
will not relax their hold on the rocks.

Some of us have to be ready—
the big winter can come back, and only
bushes from Mongolia will survive.

# BRIAN SWANN

## SOLO

At dawn, the heron revives the lake.
Water is locked round his feet.

Lingering nocturnal light is like
air in snow. The thin rain

funnels into the music of vacancy
and dies. Afternoon might be

the vivid watchfulness I have seen
stab houses, withdraw, and be

sacred again flooding roofs.
It helps, knowing nobody.

The empty highway may be thirsty
as the sea. It has left the back

of the world. Anything could be
prominent on it and remain hypnotized

in the glare of tarmac. My eyes strain
as if trying to change something.

I could disappear right now, as
the heron this morning entered

his reflection, and no repercussions
spread across the lake.

# MARGOT TREITEL

## THE BLUE OX

In his dream he is getting off the boat,
making his fortune, folding
the well-thumbed manifesto in his pocket.
So the streets aren't gold and the claims
wildly exaggerated. Still he is here,
his body a dumb animal, his soul his own.
All through the first long winter
with this thick blue snow, he sees
the enormous beast before him—loyal,
eager to please.
Each footstep a lake of sky-blue water,
each day a mile of forest cleared. Soon
he is doing the work of a thousand men,
pulling a plow through the wilderness.
A man could live like this
in these hills, axing the woods
into gardens, selling the quarter acres for a song.

# DAVID WAGONER

## A REMARKABLE EXHIBITION

> *Its diving ability in dodging at the flash of a gun*
> *is well known. I once saw a remarkable exhibition*
> *of this power by a loon which was surrounded by gunners*
> *in a small cove on the Taunton River.*
> —Arthur Cleveland Bent
> *Life Histories of North American*
> *Diving Birds,* 1919

It was remarkable, that day on the river
When eight gentlemen hunters in tweeds and gaiters,
Some firmly on shore and some wading through rushes,
Put a loon to the test.
A light mist hovered in shreds, but for all intents
It was a commonplace morning, sunlit and windless,
Affording a clear view of the clear water
And its reflective surface.
Their rifles were bench-sighted, their aim steady,
And though they varied as marksmen from indifferent
To expert, when the loon appeared out of nowhere
Beside them suddenly
At such close range, it seemed impossible
A bird of its size could dodge so many bullets
From unforeseeable angles more than a moment.
Across that cove
The sound of their guns went crackling and echoing
Under the pines, reechoing and colliding
Like the eccentric ripples that broke reflections
Around the loon's white breast
And starry back. It lifted its dark neck
And darker head and beak to go arching under,
And every time it plunged, they thought it was dying,
But it would rise
Again whole minutes later unnaturally
Far off, unexpectedly, in unpredictable
Directions, breathe, swivel and arch to dive
Again, and be gone.
They were genuinely amazed at a performance
That round for round matched theirs. It lasted longer
Than any of them could agree on through that winter

77

Over their hearthstones
When they recounted the tale and their cartridges
And tried to guess the mechanics of its defense
Aside from stubbornness and webfooted power
And those amber eyes
They couldn't help recollecting: how could they see
Magically enough to avoid eight rifles flashing
As long as all that and still, as they finally were,
Be closed in death?


# THRESHOLDS

High on the reef, the chalk-dry barnacles
In wait for sea-spray when the moon closes.

At the edge of tundra, the last leaves shading moss.
On the mountain, ice-blue gentians beside ice.

At the still of night, where death stirs like a dreamer
With eyelids shut and trembling, the mind's eye staring.

## FOR A FISHERMAN WHO DYNAMITED
## A CORMORANT ROOKERY

Lean at your rail. Look close at the ripe water.
You've lived on it and off it, but now
Slip over and settle
Down in that world where your gillnet or purse seine
Or trolling lures have been going *for* you.
Neck stretched, eyes open,
Your lubber's feet both paddling as well as they can
At a slant, deeper and deeper, your arms
Held stiff at your sides,
Your nose thrust to a point, do your best to follow
The wake of a better fisherman
Than you, the flight
Of the sleek swift cormorant plunging under the sea
At his labors, his weavings, his sudden
Changes of course beyond you
As he darts and lunges, then rises to the sun
With the rest of his short life
Quicksilver while he lifts
His slim blue-throated neck and his catch to the sky.
But stay where you are. Sink further. Enjoy
The depths of rapture
Like other divers and sailors cast adrift
Under these waves. You've been here
Before, remember:
The salt of the earth and the old salt of the ocean —
On both sides of your skin they whisper
And turn to each other.
Though you act like a stranger, you have nothing to fear
From the fish around you. Like birds of passage
They're yours alone
Just as you thought. They're finally all yours.
They'll help you to balance that good nature,
To give your share
Of the wealth to mother-of-pearl and living spirals,
To put stars gently in your place,
To change your mind
By a sea change through which everything is forgiven,
Not given up for lost, not even
You disappearing.

# INGRID WENDT

## STONE

Small as a molar, wisdom tooth
smooth and rootless, wild
rose color milky as taffy, this

delicate stone I find in the gravel
I bless, hold to the light, a treasure out
of filler material dirt depends on, becoming a road,

having already blessed each day without thinking of road
builders, for weeks my solitude deep
in the side of the Sangre de Cristos so complete

coyotes in broad daylight visit my meadow,
eagles roost unalarmed above. Territorial, only
the rufous hummingbird somehow I thought I should feed.

I never thought about gravel: where
it must come from—the side of some other mountain
gawking forever where once there was only a yawn.

Yaquina Head, back home, where once a year Murre,
proper as penguins, relinquish the waves to nest.
Rock the bill in Washington last Spring failed to save.

Stone I hold in my hand, place on my bookshelf,
light, the color of dawn, the end
of some other solitude, once more traveling on.

# ROBERTA HILL WHITEMAN

## OF LIGHT, WATER AND GATHERED DUST

Above Chequamegon Bay
two immense assemblies of summer clouds
collide, flare with messages,
and rumble their rejection.
With massive strides, they
edge each other. Bunch-backed by a load
of cauliflower, the eastern front
drives daggers of rain
into the dove-grey water
between them.

The western flyers snap green whips,
forcing cruise ships home.
When the lightning flashes,
you name a shore hovering
in mid-air. Other islands out there
are shrewd as submerging monsters,
eyes flickering in the dusk.

The gulls' transparent cries
are blown along a low cliff.
Wings awry from wind,
they read it, then balance again,
swinging like pendants beyond us.
Crickets resist the wind and sing.

Orange and red lightning
explodes in dizzy loops. Two flashes
zig from top down cloud.
The bay surges over rocks,
its fish aware of an upper world.

"Look!" I say. "In that flash, the oak grove
we walked through last spring."
Crickets approve, sing louder than before.
As shreds of cauliflower fall earthward,
houselights on Madeleine Island dim.

Above the scattering clouds,
Jupiter, close as the motel door,
and the Milky Way, no longer remote,
but bright as your laughter in the dark.
The footprints of souls who walked
this earth plane whirl toward us,
through us, beyond us, into us.

Born of light, water
and gathered dust, we grope
for one another's hand,
and trust the galaxy's embrace,
as leaves trust air, as thunder, its cloud.

You fling your cigarette over the rail.
It grows a tail and travels
through a slow, glowing arc.
For that moment,
even crickets pause.

# DAVID WILLIAMS

## OUTDOOR MOVIES AT THE STATE PARK

It's not that the people watching the movie
instead of the moon as it rises
over Lake Champlain have no souls.
It's just that, in this expanse of water
and plain the glacier left
like a great calm after great suffering,
our eyes are drawn to any
bright flickering human thing.

That's why we kneel before charcoal grills
and offer our daily news.
That's why the children in their pastel clothes
seem to gather the last of the light to themselves
and give it back—voices bright, flickering.

Two orange life-jackets glow through the dusk—
father and daughter in a canoe
borne up by a transparent mystery.
In her eyes, he's a legend—
back straight, kneeling,
holding his paddle above the lake,
drops falling from the blade
like a blessing returned. He knows
they're safe now. Failure and compromise
don't matter until they reach shore.

# CAROLYNE WRIGHT

## THE LOVELIEST COUNTRY OF OUR LIVES

The trains crawl from the stations
slow as the locomotives
in last century's tintypes.
North Dakota stretches away, a long dream
of wheat. We sleep as the cars hurtle
forward between fields and the memory
of fields . . .
        At Glendive we awaken,
stare into the moon-dry arroyos
as if for the question our dreams
kept trying all afternoon to ask,
like passengers who gesture through
plate glass to children smiling
and shrugging from the platform.

The question had something to do
with buttes rising and falling
like waves of an inland sea,
the warm Pleiocene of our recollection:

What was it we were going to become?

The cottonwood leaves go on quaking,
nodding agreement with every assertion
of the wind. The question blends imperceptibly
with its answer like a life continuing,
an ocean of fields being slowly drained
of wheat.

We shift position, the moon
fixed in mid-heaven, instructing travelers
in the reliability of light. The train
crosses the Missouri on its steel trestle;
the water is rippling and wheat-colored,
a dream of river with an answer
for every memory of fields.

        We are passing
through the loveliest country of our lives.

# CHARLES WRIGHT

## SUNDAY AT HOME
## AT THE BEGINNING OF APRIL

Spring like smoke in the fruit trees,
Ambulance siren falling away
                              through the thick grass.
I gaze at the sky and add lines to my long poem.

Truth's an indefinite article.
When we live, we live for the last time,
                              as Akhmatova says.
One *the* in a world of *a*.

# RAY A. YOUNG BEAR

## MY GRANDMOTHER'S WORDS (AND MINE) ON THE LAST SPRING BLIZZARD

The snow has fallen in variations.
Each variation has a meaning
which goes back to our *Creation*.
This morning, for instance,
branches broke under
the wet snow's weight.

Last night, in the snowstorm,
anyone could've gotten lost.

Such was the time before
our moment when the Good
eluded Evil . . .

(Despite a winter of doubt,
I owe my existence to the ally
who now rests on the ground outside
with his brilliant white blanket
covering the green grass-shoots
of another year.)

# ED ZAHNISER

## ACID RAIN

Upriver, handymen sell their houses back to Strout Realty.
Eyeball enough un-plumb jambs and rolling floors
and you can sniff apocalypse some distance off.

Here in the floodplain, sandbags sell dear.
Fishermen line their boats on rings that slide
up and down tall poles struck deep to the river's bed.

Reverend Osgood preachifies that apocalypse
is the launching pad of good theology. Even so,
they know the river's rising. They know
you'd best get yourself to higher ground.
Even the earthworms have started clearing out, Salamanca says.
Let them that have eyes to see, see.

The reverend tries to teach the kids to whistle up
the separate syllables of *eschatology*.
"Put it all together later," he says.
Salamanca says, no way. They think it's just
one more spitball needs ducking in this life.
Let them that have ears to hear, hear.

Letitia McBride tells Salamanca last night's warm winds
blew from the wrong direction. Evil, she says. Such winds.
They enter your barn door and lift the whole shebang
clean off the ground. Letitia suspects
that wasn't what Malachi meant—was it?—about God
flinging open heaven's windows. Salamanca says, "Repent.
It's the tenth portion that anchors your barn."

# CONTRIBUTORS

**PHILIP APPLEMAN** lives in Sagaponack, New York, and is author of *Apes and Angels* (Putnam) and *Darwin's Ark* (Indiana University Press). His work has appeared in the *Nation, Poetry,* and elsewhere.

**CHARLES ATKINSON** teaches writing at the University of California, Santa Cruz. His poetry has appeared in magazines around the country, including *Poetry, Virginia Quarterly Review,* and *Poetry Northwest.* He is a recent recipient of both the Stanford and Crolier prizes for poetry.

**JIM BARNES** edits *The Chariton Review* at Northeast Missouri State University. His most recent books of poetry are *A Season of Loss* and *La Plata Cantata* (Purdue University Press).

**MARVIN BELL** teaches at the University of Iowa and lives part of each year in Port Townsend, Washington. He is the author of nine books of poetry, a collection of essays, and, with William Stafford, two volumes of poems written as correspondence. Atheneum published his *New and Collected Poems* in 1987. Copper Canyon will publish a new collection, *Iris of Creation,* in 1990.

**WENDELL BERRY** lives and farms in Port Royal, Kentucky. He is author of *A Part, The Wheel,* and *The Collected Poems of Wendell Berry: 1957-1982* (North Point Press). His fiction (*A Place on Earth, Nathan Coulter,* and *The Wild Birds*) and essays (*The Gift of Good Land, Recollected Essays 1965-1980, Standing By Words,* and *Home Economics*) are also available from North Point Press. He is a recipient of the Jean Stein Award from the American Academy and Institute of Arts and Letters.

**SALLIE BINGHAM** is a native of the Ohio River Valley, lives outside Louisville, and writes fiction, poetry, and plays. She is coeditor of the *American Voice,* and her latest book, a memoir entitled *Passion and Prejudice,* was published by Alfred Knopf in 1989.

**PETER BLUE CLOUD** is a Turtle Mohawk from Caughnawaga, and a former ironworker. He has served as editor of the *Alcatraz Newsletter,* poetry editor of *Akwesasne Notes,* and coeditor of *Coyote's Journal.* He has published six books, including *Elderberry Flute Song* and *White Corn Sister.*

**PHILIP BOOTH** lives in Maine and "writes from there out into the world." He is author of eight books of poetry, including *Selves,* just published by Viking.

**PETER BORRELLI** lives in Vischer Ferry, New York, and is editor of *The Amicus Journal*. He writes poetry occasionally on ecological themes to prove how difficult it is.

**FRED CHAPPELL** teaches at the University of North Carolina, Greensboro, North Carolina. His latest book of poems is *First and Last Words* (Louisiana State University Press). His latest novel is *Brighten the Corner Where You Are* (St. Martin's Press).

**ALFRED CORN** lives in New York City. He is author of five volumes of poetry. The most recent, *The West Door*, was published by Viking Penguin.

**JOHN DANIEL** lives in Portland, Oregon, and teaches at the Northwest Writing Institute. *Common Ground*, his first book of poems, was published in 1989 by Confluence Press. His poems, essays, and articles have appeared in the *Southern Review*, *Poetry*, *Orion Nature Quarterly*, the *North American Review*, and other magazines.

**JEANNINE DOBBS** lives in Merrimack, New Hampshire. Her publications include articles on women writers, the teaching of writing, and American and British literature. Her poetry has appeared in numerous literary magazines and anthologies.

**GENE FRUMKIN** teaches at the University of New Mexico. A collection of long poems entitled *Comma in the Ear* will be published soon by the Living Batch Press and distributed by the University of New Mexico Press. A volume of his selected poems also will be published soon by Cinco Puntos Press.

**BRENDAN GALVIN** lives in Durham, Connecticut. He recently published a book-length poem, *Wampanoag Traveler* (Louisiana State University Press), about an eighteenth-century American naturalist, and a collection of poems entitled *Great Blue* (University of Illinois Press). He is currently a Guggenheim Fellow.

**XU GANG** is author of six collections of poems. He works for the *People's Daily* in China. **DENNIS DING** (translator) is a native of Gunyang and teaches English at Guizhou Normal University. **EDWARD MORIN** (translator) teaches English at Wayne State University.

**ALBERT GOLDBARTH** lives in Wichita, Kansas, and teaches at Wichita State University. Recent collections of his writing include a book of poems entitled *Popular Culture* (Ohio State University Press) and a collection of essays entitled *A Sympathy of Souls* (Coffee House Press).

**PATRICK WORTH GRAY** lives in Bellevue, Nebraska. He is author of *Spring Comes Again to Arnett* (Mr. Cogito Press) and *Disappearances* (University of Nebraska Press).

**JOHN HAINES** lives in Fairbanks, Alaska, where he has been a homesteader for many years. His poems have appeared in such periodicals as the *Nation, Hudson Review, Massachusetts Review,* and *Poetry.* He was awarded the Massachusetts Review Prize for poetry in 1965, a Guggenheim Fellowship in 1965, and a grant from the National Endowment for the Arts in 1967. His latest book of poems, *New Poems, 1980-88,* will be published soon by Story Line Press.

**DONALD HALL** lives in Danbury, New Hampshire. His books of poems include *Exiles and Marriages, The Dark Houses, A Roof of Tiger Lilies, The Alligator Bride,* and *The Yellow Room Love Poems.* He won the Lamont Poetry Selection in 1955 and was awarded a Guggenheim Fellowship in 1963.

**JIM HARRISON** lives in Lake Leelanau, Michigan. His latest book is *The Woman Lit by Fireflies* published by Houghton Mifflin. Formerly he was the poetry editor of the *Nation.*

**JANE HIRSHFIELD** lives in Mill Valley, California. She is author of two books of poetry. She has received a Guggenheim Fellowship, the Commonwealth Club of California's Poetry Medal, a Columbia University Translation Center Award, and other honors. Her work has appeared in the *New Yorker,* the *Atlantic,* the *American Poetry Review,* and the *Paris Review.*

**BEN HOWARD** teaches in the Division of Humanities at Alfred University, Alfred, New York. He is author most recently of *Lenten Anniversaries: Poems 1982-85* (Cummington Press). His work has appeared in *Poetry,* the *Kenyon Review,* the *Sewanee Review,* and elsewhere.

**DAVID IGNATOW** lives in New York City. He is author of fourteen volumes of poetry, including *Poems: 1934-69* and *New and Collected Poems: 1970-1985.* Another volume, *Despite the Plainness: Love Poems,* will be published shortly. He is president emeritus of the Poetry Society of America and professor emeritus of the City University of New York. His poetry prizes include a Bollingen Prize, a Wallace Stevens Fellowship, and a Shelley Memorial Award.

**GEORGE KEITHLEY** lives in Chico, California. His epic poem *The Donner Party* was a Book-of-the-Month Club selection, received the Western Heritage Award, and has been adapted as a play and an opera. His *Song in a Strange Land* received the Di Castagnola Award from the Poetry Society of America.

**MAXINE KUMIN** lives in Warner, New Hampshire. Her books of poetry include *Nurture, In Deep,* and *The Long Approach* (Viking).

**SYDNEY LEA** lives in Orford, New Hampshire, and teaches writing at Vermont College. He is founder and former editor of the *New England Review/Bread Loaf Quarterly* and author of four collections of poetry, most recently *Prayer for the Little City.* A member of the National Environmental Leadership Council, he is currently working on his second novel and a collection of naturalist essays.

**DENISE LEVERTOV** lives in Seattle, Washington, and teaches every winter at Stanford University. Her books of poetry include *Here and Now, Overland to the Islands, With Eyes at the Back of Our Heads, The Jacob's Ladder, O Taste and See!, The Sorrow Dance,* and *Relearning the Alphabet.* Her most recent book was *A Door in the Hive* (New Directions).

**PETER MEINKE** lives in St. Petersburg, Florida, where he is director of the Writing Workshop at Eckerd College. His latest book, *Night Watch on the Chesapeake,* was published in 1987 by the Pitt Poetry Series. His book *The Piano Tuner* won the 1986 Flannery O'Connor Award for Short Fiction.

**W. S. MERWIN** lives in Hawaii, where he is active in the campaign to protect rain forests. He is author of fourteen books of poetry. In 1970 he won a Pulitzer Prize for *The Carrier of Ladders.* He received the 1987 Governor's Award for Literature from the State of Hawaii for his most recent work, *The Rain in the Trees* (Alfred Knopf).

**ROGER MITCHELL** teaches at Indiana University in Bloomington. His books of poetry include *Adirondack, Letters from Siberia and Other Poems, Moving,* and *A Clear Space on a Cold Day.* His essays and reviews have appeared in *American Book Review,* the *Ohio Review, American Poetry Review, Prairie Schooner, Indiana Review,* and elsewhere.

**RUTH MOOSE** lives in Albemarle, North Carolina. Her poetry has appeared in the *Atlantic,* the *Ohio Review, Prairie Schooner,* and the *New York Times.*

**DUANE NIATUM** lives in Seattle, Washington, and is author of four volumes of poetry, including *Songs for the Harvester of Dreams* (University of Washington Press), which won the 1982 National Book Award from the Before Columbus Foundation. He is a member of the Klamath tribe, whose ancestral lands are on the Washington coast.

**JULIA OLDER** lives in Hancock, New Hampshire. Her most recent collection of poetry is entitled *A Little Wild*.

**MARY OLIVER** lives in Provincetown, Massachusetts. Her most recent book is *House of Light*, published by Beacon Press. Her other books include *Twelve Moons, Dream Work*, and *American Primitive*, for which she received the Pulitzer Prize in 1984.

**JOSÉ EMILIO PACHECO** was born in Mexico City and has won many distinguished awards, including the Premio Nacional de Poesía. In addition to his numerous books of poetry, he is author of two novels, several collections of short stories, screenplays, essays, and translations. **LINDA SCHEER** (translator) lives in Brooklyn, New York. She is coeditor and cotranslator of *Poetry of Transition: Mexican Poetry of the '60s and '70s*.

**JAROLD RAMSEY** lives in Rochester, New York, and teaches at the University of Rochester. For the past twelve years his scholarship has focused on identifying and understanding American Indian literature. His books of poetry include *Love in an Earthquake, Dermographia*, and *Hand-Shadows*, which won a Quarterly Review of Literature Poetry Prize for 1989.

**PAUL ROCHE** is a poet, novelist, and translator, who lives on the island of Majorca in Spain.

**NORMAN H. RUSSELL** lives in Edmond, Oklahoma, and is retired from teaching university biology and poetry. He is part Cherokee, and much of his work, which has appeared in thirteen chapbooks and many magazines, reflects Native American values and respect for the natural world.

**REG SANER** teaches at the University of Colorado in Boulder. He is author of many books of poetry, including *So This Is the Map* (Random House) and *Climbing into the Roots*, a Walt Whitman award winner. His work has appeared in the *Georgia Review, Ironwood*, and elsewhere. He has trained at the U.S. Army's Arctic Indoctrination and Survival School in Alaska and is currently writing a collection of essays exploring nature in the American West.

**TERRENCE SAVOIE** lives in Davenport, Iowa. His work has appeared in *Poetry*, the *Iowa Review*, the *Black Warrior Review*, and the *American Poetry Review*.

**SUSAN FROMBERG SHAEFFER** lives in Brooklyn, New York, and in London, England, and teaches English at Brooklyn College. She has written eight novels and five volumes of poetry, including *Granite Lady* and *The Bible of the Beasts of the Little Field*.

**GARY SNYDER** lives in the foothills of the California Sierra. He has just finished a prose book on wilderness and culture entitled *The Practice of the Wild*. His poetry books in print include *Myths & Texts*, *The Back Country*, *Regarding Wave*, *Earth House Hold*, and *Turtle Island*, for which he received the Pulitzer Prize in 1975.

**KATHLEEN SPIVACK** lives in Watertown, Massachusetts. She directs the Advanced Writing Workshop in Cambridge and is author of four books of poems, including *The Beds We Lie In* (Scarecrow Press), a 1986 Pulitzer Prize nominee. Her poetry has appeared in the *New Yorker*, *Poetry*, the *Atlantic*, *Ironwood*, *Antaeus*, the *Paris Review*, *Prairie Schooner*, and *Harper's*.

**WILLIAM STAFFORD** lives in Lake Oswego, Oregon. A former poetry consultant for the Library of Congress, his poetry and prose have appeared in numerous publications. His most recent books of poetry are *Writing the World* (Alembic Press), *A Scripture of Leaves* (The Brethren Press), and *Fin, Feather, Fur* (Honeybrook Press). In 1962 his collection of poems entitled *Traveling Through the Dark* won a National Book Award for poetry.

**BRIAN SWANN** lives in New York City, where he teaches at The Cooper Union for the Advancement of Science and Art. He has published many volumes of poetry, fiction, poetry in translation, and has edited three volumes on Native American literature. He is also director of the Bennington Writing Workshops and poetry editor of the *Amicus Journal*.

**MARGOT TREITEL** lives in Columbia, Maryland. Her poem "The Blue Ox" appeared in her chapbook, *The Inside Story*, which won the 1987 Artscape Literary Arts Competition sponsored by the City of Baltimore. Her work has also appeared in the *Chicago Review*, the *Prairie Schooner*, and *College English*.

**DAVID WAGONER** lives in Seattle, Washington, where he edits *Poetry Northwest* and teaches at the University of Washington. He has written more than a dozen books of poetry and ten novels. His most recent book of poems is *Through the Forest: New and Selected Poems 1977-1987* (Atlantic Monthly Press).

**INGRID WENDT** lives in Eugene, Oregon. Her poem "Stone" was written while she was in residence at the D.H. Lawrence Ranch outside Taos, New Mexico, as the recipient of the 1982 D.H. Lawrence Award. She is author of two books of poems, *Moving the House* and *Singing the Mozart Requiem* (Breitenbush Books), and winner of the 1988 Oregon Book Award for Poetry.

**ROBERTA HILL WHITEMAN** lives in St. Paul, Minnesota, and teaches at the University of Wisconsin. She is an Oneida Indian and has written a collection of poems entitled *Star Quilt* (Holy Cow! Press).

**DAVID WILLIAMS** lives in Worcester, Massachusetts. His poems have appeared in the *Atlantic, Beloit Poetry Journal, Harbor Review, Poetry East,* and *Sonora Review.* In 1984, he received a fellowship from the Massachusetts Council for the Arts. At various times he has taught elementary school, adult basic education, and college English, and is active in refugee support work.

**CAROLYNE WRIGHT** lives in Seattle, Washington. She is author of four volumes of poetry, among them *Stealing the Children* (Ahsahta Press) and *Premonitions of an Uneasy Guest* (AWP Award Series). She has held Fulbright grants to Chile and Bangladesh and an Indo-U.S. Subcommission Fellowship to Calcutta. A volume of translations of Chilean poet Jorge Teillier is forthcoming from the University ot Texas Press.

**CHARLES WRIGHT** lives in Charlottesville, Virginia, and teaches at the University of Virginia. He has published several books of poetry, most recently *Zone Journals. The World of the 10,000 Things* will be published in 1990. In addition, he has translated two volumes of Italian poetry.

**RAY A. YOUNG BEAR** is a Mesquakie (People of the Red Earth) poet from Tama, Iowa. His first collection of poems was published in 1980 by Harper & Row. His second collection, *The Invisible Musician,* was released in February 1990 by Holy Cow! Press of Duluth, Minnesota.

**ED ZAHNISER** lives in Shepherdstown, West Virginia. A former poetry editor of *Living Wilderness,* he now edits and produces *Arts and Kulchur of the Mountain State,* a supplement to *Mountain Pathways,* West Virginia's only statewide independent environmental publication. His poetry and short fiction have appeared in literary magazines in the United States and the United Kingdom.